BLUE MOUND TO 161

GARIN CYCHOLL

Winner of the 2003-04 Transcontinental Poetry Award

BLUE MOUND TO 161

GARIN CYCHOLL

PAVEMENT SAW PRESS
OHIO

Editor & Layout: David Baratier
Associate Editor: Sean Karns
Duck Logo: Joe Napora
Cover art: Lance King

Passages of this poem previously appeared in Mudlark.

Pavement Saw Press
PO Box 6291
Columbus, OH 43206
pavementsaw.org

Ohio Arts Council
A STATE AGENCY
THAT SUPPORTS PUBLIC
PROGRAMS IN THE ARTS

Products are available through the publisher or through:
SPD / 1341 Seventh St. / Berkeley, CA 94710 / 510.524.1668

Winner of the 2003-4 Transcontinental Poetry Award for an out-
standing first book-length collection of poetry or prose as chosen by
Judith Vollmer, who deserves our loudest huzzah! We read yearly
from June 1st until August 15th. Send an SASE for information.

Pavement Saw Press is a not for profit corporation, any donations
are greatly appreciated and are considered as charitable tax
donations under section 501(c) of the federal tax code.

FOR MICHAEL ANANIA

". . .In the picture, Elizabeth is eight years old. She wants me to know, she says, how people used to live in these small settlements down in Wayne County. She wants me to notice that there are no wild animals in the picture. Out of breath, she and her cousins are frozen in play. Their eyes laugh at the camera, like they're seeking permission to begin their game again. 'Her—' Elizabeth points, 'she's passed on.' Fence lines. Flecks in the sky. A fold in the picture. The corners of two outbuildings. I point. 'The northwest corner of Pilgrim Holiness church,' she says. 'The creek is just out of the picture.'"

Blue Mound to 161

into the south of it
      (*Illinois*
how from any road, Geff
seemed south to me
Wayne City, too
not the crux or
"at the center" but

       on this side
       on that side

not even "border states"
then but roomfuls of voices
debating secession in
Union and Alexander
downstate counties Federal
guns already come down
from Chicago to hold the
rivers at Cairo

*armed forces
in chicago*

        or trucks
crossing the bridge there
Corollas running I-24 into
Kentucky Cadillacs flying
I-57 north   coal barges
slipping locks, dodging
catfishermen tanker cars
of acids passing through
the East St. Louis yards
these things' momentum

*trucks crossing
natural supplies into
East St Louis
yards.*

staggering

       these girls
singing in place their
songs testing the memory

*singing
of
memory*

     in rocks
     in sedges

in seeds
in the reptile itself

as the song says, *looking*
at my own bad
attitude toward the
pastoral the *here-*
ness of it ground
measured out in
spoil heaps and

the world begins
in a ditch—light, air,
aluminum, water—
no quack grasses, these
yellowfruit sedge, cuplike
and sick-brown, blooms
hidden, nerves running
the convex face "The only
station in Southern Illinois
for this grass is a wet ditch
near the junction of Illinois
highways 3 and 144."

Three Jonesboro girls in a field,
dancing to the static of blue transistors.

"Play your radio, play!" one girl sings,
her knee skinned from scooping a volleyball

on a school gymnasium floor. With long arms,
a second tugs loose stems of Joe Pye Weed,

holds them aloft. The third smacks her dirt-
singed palm to ground and three solos begin.

O gymnasium songs!
O songs in a girl's knee and wrist!

O handheld blue plastic songs!
O songs in a Jonesboro field!

Song of Three Jonesboro Girls in a Field

"Blessed is my maker! He brought
the mound and the greasy flowers and
this Joe Pye weed! He pulls it up
and plants it! I'm his handmaid."

"Blessed's not your maker. Blessed is
my maker. He come to town in a '67
Plymouth. Sold catfish and live box-
heads out the back. Profit's his name!"

"Face it, girls. Blessed is one long
gone motherfucker. He's gone walking
down Route 13. Taken the ferry at Cave-
in-Rock and he won't be back no more."

Make no mistake! We are going to get Andrew
Johnson!

Mother, I am now a guerilla in every sense of
the word, going upriver to kidnap the Vice President
of the United States. Our boat is a fine one, the
Rachel. She is ex-Yankee, confiscated and brought
to Memphis by a group of desperate men one year ago.
Days, we navigate nearest the banks, moving from
shadow to shadow. We drill on the nine-inch
Dahlgren astern. The captain orders us about. He
is afraid of the Yankee guns at Cairo. He says,
'General Pillow is a violent man. He would sooner
see us dead. We must be ready.'

I am sick to death of snakes. This river is
full of them. They swim along the banks and hull,
drop from tree limbs. Them and snappers. Flicker
said that there are turtles in this river who are
bigger than small dogs. The chaplain said that yes,
and people who live along the river sometimes wor-
ship these reptiles as gods. Flicker said that this
was untrue. When the other man argued, the men took
Flicker's part, then carried the chaplain below
deck, giving him the old what-for.

Nights, we moor in the shallows along the
western bank. Porter plays his fiddle and we chase
the Missouri girls back up into the woods.

(a million yrs ago   the Gulf
sucked down to the Delta   leaving deep swamp
plantings of one-thousand-year trees—Tupe-
los and Swamp Cypress   *adhering to stumps,*
Cypress Knee sedges, stout and blacklike. . .
meadowbeauties and Asa Gray   the Cache
seeps from Little Black Slough into flat water
below the Dongola-Cypress Blacktop

Lieutenant Culp hollers and we run circles around the deck. Sometimes the Captain comes out and fires his pistol randomly into the water. When he hits a turtle, he shouts, "Ah ha!"

Then, the Lieutenant asks, "Isn't anyone going in to get the Captain his lunch?"

Yesterday, I leaped into the water, wrestling a fifteen-pound snapper to the top.

I heard the Captain's voice through the water, "Keep that reptile from sinking!"

When I was back on deck, the Lieutenant said, "You're a good man. What's your name again?"

After lunch, we ran more circles around the deck.

This is what we do when Lieutenant Culp hollers.

Flicker and I drew night watch. He asked me, "How long do you think it takes to get to Louisville anyway?"

I told him that I didn't know.

Flicker laughed. He asked, "Do you trust the captain? Can you trust a man who's paid twenty-five dollars a day?"

After watch, Porter played his fiddle and we chased the Missouri girls back up into the woods.

". . .It is thought that these Gulf Coastal Plain species have not come into Southern Illinois by extending their ranges to the north but, on the contrary, are survivors of a great association of plants that flourished here in the remote past. . .The Bald Cypress attains a large size in swamps of Alexander and Pulaski counties, but in Jackson County, it grows only to a moderate height (25-28 m.) and is less frequently found. It is planted extensively by the Illinois State Highway Department."

"Andrew Johnson is sitting down to a hotel breakfast, and all we have to eat is what we pull out of this river," Flicker says. He works his skillet.

Mother, he keeps it good and greasy. But he complains. It puts me in a mind to get to Cairo as soon as possible. He complains about the drills, the fish and reptiles. He complains about things I don't even understand. This afternoon, I was on deck watching the scenery along the river pass.

Flicker came up and said, "Why do you think they call them banks?"

What was I supposed to say to that? I am tired of this river. I have a skin rash. Flicker says that it comes of eating too many reptiles. I have a mind to ask the Lieutenant to detach me from this vessel and order me to sea. But all he'd say is, "You know your place, boy?"

We moor again along the shallows. Porter plays his fiddle and we chase the Missouri girls back up into the woods. Although with less enthusiasm. Mother, how large is Missouri?

Our county data are largely based on the literature and confirmed sightings, but plants do move and not all populations have been documented. Significant gaps in the map distribution may not be real.

At night, the men talked on deck. The river's dark.

"What do you know about Andrew Johnson anyway?" Flicker asked.

The men shook their heads.

"Don't you think it's strange that we're being paid to go capture a man we don't know nothing about," Flicker said.

"I know that he's a son of a bitch," Culp growled.

"You know that because you are being paid ten dollars and us five."

I hesitate to even write this down.

Flicker came to me in the night.

"Wake up," he said. "I have figured out why we're still in Missouri."

He took me out on deck, pointed to the trees on the bank. They drifted backwards in the moonlight.

"Culp comes up each night and pulls up the anchor. We drift back downriver each night. We'll never get to fucken Cairo. Let alone Louisville—"

Lieutenant Culp came along.

"What are you men doing up?" he asked.

We said nothing and went back to our bedrolls.

"Days, I've been marking trees," Flicker whispered. "We've passed the same catalpas five, six days in a row. The captain is afraid of General Pillow. We are stuck here on this river for the rest of the war. Unless we—"

He said more, but I didn't listen. Flicker is a good man. He cooks for us. But I've come to listen less and less to him. I waited for the breakfast bell, the chance to run again on deck.

Mother, I miss your biscuits. I am tired of eating turtles.

before the streets whole
dislocations or coasts gone
south *Cottus Carolinae* still
swimming southern conduits
blind fish entering caves (*in
them*, whole morphological
changes)   or Hicks Dome
(el. 677 ft.) shattered sedi-
mentary rock seeping with
igneous activity one of 8
craters in a line from Rose
Dome, Kansas

                    *I have heard
suggestions that the dome
resulted from a meteorite, but
its surficial and underground
structure indicates that the
forces that formed it came
from below rather than above*

(behind them, empty fields

flashlit handful of line
flecked with pond water
Herb drags the turtle up
at 2 A.M. tries to recall
that guy's name on Scuda-
more who pays you fifty
cents a shell

we are going down to the lake
                    down to the lake
                    down to the lake   false goats-
beard and smoke trees along the dam Jack's voice
hung in the branches   *two on*
                    two out

fishbones in the woods
turtle's mouth rises at two o'clock
green water scummed down
by the flashlight   line strung
with a fistful of chicken liver and
motherfucker's his mouth opens
and closes with the knife

"Throw the shell in the weeds!
Throw the head in the pond!"

"Take my picture, Herb! The knife's
in the cabin. Watch the broken glass
on the porch! Can you hear the neighbors?
Are they singing?"

                    Mrs. Brooks,
Mrs. Brooks! If Mrs. Brooks ate turtles,
we'd all be millionaires.

   rusted sawtooth
buried next to the catalpa (3 qts. of
melted ice cream and Glen Henson's
outdated beans)   all of us out here
running away   eating cold chicken
by the light of the moon

it was very south, he sd
measure the distance in
miles or bits of song
across rivers through
seasons *these things'*
momentum staggering
seeds spread by air, bird
or flood floating on
random storms *gods*
dwindled in the talk of it
furious motion on both
sides of the river but *here*
at the center? *no* motions
slowing to *non* the girls'
idyll the yards working
precise movements bills
of lading   *lasted for*
seconds, then was
gone

(down to the caves

Nature is
Conspiracy
why do they call banks, banks?

Song of Three Jonesboro Girls in a Field

"The ground thickens and blacks. Quick,
man! Grab your shovel and pick! Your
helmet, light and yellowbird! Follow the
waters. Go into the earth!"

"While maidens gather stones in fields, we
are going into the earth. Into the earth. In-
to the earth! Archimedes Cave lies under
the rock. Come back, yellowbird!"

"Yellowbird'll be back tomorrow. Gathering
is hard on my knees. Gather your own stones,
old men. We are going into the ground, toting
bouquets of yellow dog's teeth and mayapples."

Soft-coal miners across the country walked out on April 1, 1922. Southern Illinois Coal Company owner William J. Lester (Cornell '01) was granted permission by local union officials to "uncover" coal, as long as he did not ship it. By early June he had 60,000 tons of coal. Lester said, "It's legal and I need the money. Why shouldn't I?"

Later, on July 11, one Williamson County resident told the *New York Herald*, "Well, you can never make me believe John Lewis intended to have anybody go out and do some killing. When Lewis officially told the strikers that those fellows out at Lester's mine were to be treated like any other strike - breakers I should say it was about the same as saying, 'Hike out there to the mine and clean 'em out.'"

Yet, on June 16, Lester notified the Burlington Railroad that 16 cars of coal were ready for shipment.

is a single channel evident?
layers of water   the Cache-Bay
riverless and swimming 15 ft. below
the level of these swamps not
prairie marshes but temporary
localities of water all draining

>   *(like jazz is made*
>   *out of what else*
>   *but other things in*
>   *the specificity of*
>   *place*

or against that layers
of silt (most falsely called
"clay") at one time the
bottom of the world
fossil prints of angio-
sperms or weeds against
sky in a ditch   detritus
black and white as a
mortician's tricks: candles
half-shirts coins razor
paste mint and thread in
the skin

>   *there is no longer a*
>   *true soil here*

Just northwest of Moake Crossing, across the Coal Belt Electric tracks and to the north of the powerhouse, was a strip of woodland, green with the fresh foliage of early summer, lush with the undergrowth of many years. Into it the mob herded its captives, the strikebreakers and company guards. In less than three hundred feet they came to a stout fence strung with four strands of barbed wire. A big bearded man in overalls with a slouch hat called out:

"Here's where you run the gauntlet. Now, damn you, let's see how fast you can run between here and Chicago, you damned gutter-bums!"

Post Creek cut sixty miles off the river. *Is a single channel evident?* If map is a measure of space, whose song goes marching over weeds? Natural channels are sinuous. The Bone Gap Opera. Who are these? If the waters are moving. If Art Sinsabaugh sets up his view camera somewhere along the Dongola blacktop. *The important thing is being portable.* Whatever moves here. If neutralizing limestone is not present, the shale gob piles will emit acids. If chronicle is a measure of time, what color is the ink? The first miners were Italian. If these weeds are found only in certain corners of the South, what brought them? Gravel is a recent addition. *Here, the vegetation may even burn in such times.*

Those still alive were taken to Herrin Hospital; the dead were sent to a vacant storeroom in the same city. There they were stripped, washed, laid on pine boxes, and covered with sheets. Then the doors were opened, and for hours men and women (often with babies in their arms) filed past. Some spat on the corpses, some said to the children whose hands they held: "Look at the dirty bums who tried to take the bread out of your mouths!"

Long before nightfall flies blackened the wounds that still seeped in the eighteen bodies.*

----

*Another body was found the following day.

scouring is from
below   o, rivers!
leaving half-moon
ponds horseshoe
washes and dead
rivers   the Embarras
Little Wabash and Big
Muddy swimming
with pollen bones and
shells Skillet Fork
swamping ground
giving way   back-
water scars residual
swamps   *an un-*
disturbed channel
is hard to find in
Illinois

(this savage land

I am watching the sun rise
in Cairo, Illinois. Over my
shoulder, she says,
                    There
ain't fuck to do here if you
ain't geography.

                    I say,
Let's take some pictures. I'll
take some barn shots of you.
The light should just be getting
good.

          You think I'd trust
myself to your fat, red fingers?
You think that I want to be one
of your Jonesboro girls in a field
near Little Grassy Lake?

                    Please?

Take your own goddamned
picture.

          Do you want to paint?

No.

          Wear the masks?

                    No.

Go down to the pond?

                    No.

                              Cat-
fish?

          No.

labor union

Strike, laborers

kill 18 scabs

—conspiracies for
change

-complaints

Food chains!

-

Song of Three Jonesboro Girls in a Field

"Sing a song of S. Glenn Young, noted
and sleuthy! Federal agent who tracked
three thousand Appalachian draft dodgers!
Caught no less than 27 desperadoes!"

"S. Glenn, man in a hood, man in a hurry.
No grand dragon, but corporal in a private
army, sick with accusation. The acting
law here. Star cut from tin."

"S. Glenn, *a distinct and glaring disgrace
to the service*. Bug-eared and blue-skinned.
Legs bowed from his many days in the
saddle. Eyes, an odd shade of gray."

On Saturday morning Herrin discovered that despite the presence of National Guardsmen it was in the hands of the Klan. Armed Klansmen, wearing crude stars cut from tin, patrolled the streets and kept crowds from forming, while in the city hall S. Glenn Young, calling himself acting chief of police, heard the reports of men he had sworn in as deputy policemen, directed that arrests be made, and ordered prisoners to jail. A sentry stood at the door of the office he had pre-empted, and no one who could not give the Klan's password was admitted.

the woods are moving, snakes
coming down to Winters Pond
and the Scatters shagbarks among
sloughs flecks of limestone in
their skins   cottonmouths and mud
snakes, zigzags and ground skinks,
snappers and red-eared sliders
(some burrowed here all winter)
crossing LaRue Road, leaving
their cuts in the bluffs   *Do not
pick up the snakes until you are
absolutely certain they are
poisonous.*

On the night of April 9, 1924, thousands of Klan supporters cele - brated their primary election victories by staging a motor parade that visit - ed Herrin, Johnston City, and Dewmaine, and returned to Marion to burn a huge cross—the first such demonstration in almost a year.

Four days later ten robed Klansmen marched into the Marion Methodist Church, knelt in silence while a young woman who accompanied them sang a stanza of "The Fiery Cross," and then presented the pastor with twenty-seven dollars and a letter commending him for his good work.

On May 1 several thousand attended a Klan barbecue at Herrin, burned two crosses, and initiated two hundred men and women.

Three weeks later, crowds thronged to a "Klantauqua" at Marion, and for three days listened to Klan orations relieved by entertainment in the Chatauqua manner.

"We traveled usually by motor, and if possible
by station wagon, station wagons in those
days being functional vehicles which served
as carry-alls, field laboratories, and lodging
for the night. Mostly we went by twos, some-
times by threes or fours, and though there were
many short trips, the bulk of our information
came from journeys of a thousand miles or so
which took ten days or longer. A specimen day
would start out early in the morning. We would
drive down the highway at a good clip, then at
the cry of 'Trads!' the auto would pull off beside
the road and we would tumble out to make a quick
reconnoiter of the site before setting down to our
regular routine. . ."

protector of Harrisburg scourge
of Egypt Shachnai Itzik Birger (b.
Russia 1880) Glen Carbon drifter
cowboy   distinguished service with
the 13th US Cavalry in the Philippines
then Charlie   locked down in his
Rte. 13 bunker 4-day supply of ammo
canned food and water

                                        (*Who*
was it accused the Sheltons of robbing
that postman of $21,000?   *it was*
those damned slots did it

                              good busi-
ness—running booze up to East St. Louis
(cops in their off-hours $100/mo.) running
the bottoms up through Sparta, Steeleville,
Waterloo   Charlie Birger kept a whole town
in coal that winter   drove the Sheltons to
Peoria

                          (*I never killed*
a good man

"A specimen of Dichromena latifolia Bald. is in the Southern Illinois University herbarium with the following data: Makanda, Illinois, 1872. This is from the George Hazen French collection. Since this species occurs only in the southeastern United States, we are assuming that a mix-up of labels has occurred since Mr. French did carry on an extensive exchange with southern collectors such as C. Mohr and William Harvey."

leaving Okawville on May 23 S. Glenn
Young and wife (he had married again
after his divorce) their big, black
Lincoln traveling the Kaskaskia
bottoms *a stretch dreary even in*
spring time   lonely but for a
passing Dodge and shots poured
into their big, black Lincoln she
slumped forward he stopped to
return fire   one leg useless

          (*it was Birger that did it*

Wood's was good prairie, 10 mi.
from Mt. Carmel Webb's, good land
in Franklin County, 15 mi. east of
Frankfort   Indian Prairie (10 mi.
northwest of Fairfield) had soil of
indifferent quality Nine Mile in Perry
County was low and wet—so named for

rich
undulating
surface or
thin
second-
rate
soil or its
peculiar
shape

like Oblong occupies ten sections
in Crawford County or Smith's, near
Lewiston, "a most beautiful prairie"
extending into St. Clair County, Ridge
divides the waters that fall into the
Mississippi on the west and the Kas-
kaskia on the east

(Earl Shelton replied

We aren't
given to
boasting
what great
warriors we
are — like Birger
all hemmed in
armor and machine
guns at the
Shady Rest.

(this savage land

which traveled better, religion or
moonshine?

while a black wave
on both sides
pushed out onto the land

3 bombs fell. Only one found the
Shady Rest. Charley Birger, holed
up at his roadside barbecue stand on
Rte. 13, resisting the Klan and bringing
uncut booze up from Florida to the stock-
yards, the Mounds Club and Ill-Mo Bar.
Then, Glen Young and 3 others gunned
down in a Herrin drugstore. Birger, hung
at Benton, 4/19/28, for the murder of a
state trooper and his wife. *The spectators
laughed at him and the jury took just 12
minutes to find him totally sane.* 50
Sheltons died mysteriously.

Song of Three Jonesboro Girls in a Field

"If they'd not taken that diamond ring
from Birger, there'd be peace in the city,
peace in the city. If the Sheltons hadn't
been so keen on dynamite, there'd be—"

"peace in the city, peace in the city. High
Pockets, Blackie, and Rado denying saints
the vote in Herrin. Or if Carl Shelton'd stayed
away from Helen. Newman dolled in his mink—"

"stuck a knife in his pocket and called on a prone
Carl in his hospital bed. There'd be peace in
the city. The Syrians and Italians across the
river in Missouri. The utter chaos of the scene."

Inhabitants in the Illinois Southern Hospital for the Insane at Anna

Name: *Folkonor, Frank*

> **Form of Disease:** *mania*
> **Duration of Present Attack:** *8*
> **Total # of Attacks:** *1*
> **Age at Which First Attack Occurred:** *28*
> **Length of Time in Asylum:** *6 yrs*
> **Suicidal/Homicidal:**
>> *At times seems insane. The last named is in the asylum, but has property in this place and no family.**

* United States Census, June 1880, Supplemental Schedule 1

Two kids ride

        bikes through pea

                gravel, spokes ticking

Gibson, Torre,

        Clemente. Sign

                in the window at

Harrisburg Wash-

        town: **WE DO**

                MINERS' CLOTHES

sinkhole ponds   dissolved and
fallen cave roofs   ill-tempered
snakes seeking limestone
shortleaf pines swamp loose-
strife and sourgums   in isolation
spring peepers and spotted
salamanders   "the historical
association of populations all
fucked up" *carex brachyglossa*—
veins stalk into dry spikes miles
from any coast

                    "Further study
of these ponds is needed."

McCarver's Extra-Inning Blast Sends Fans Home

(WP-Folkers. LP-Ray. T-3:23)

Jimmy
Wynn
watched
the
ball leak
over
the right
field wall   then

coming back
across the
bridge into Il-
linois, orange
lights on the
river's east
side:

PEABODY COAL

some were transplanted
from Alcatraz locked in
the control unit with
Leonard Peltier
Sekou Odinga
Ted Kaczynski
Manuel Noriega
Terry Nichols
Standing Deer
dislocated and
passing through
Greed's Ironhouse
the Fed's Supermax
at Marion, IL *can you*
hear me there, under
23 hr. lockdown?
cell 6 x 8' window
42 x 4" a black-
and-white TV set
showing closed-circuit
classes in psychology
education anger
management parenting
literacy *even religious*
services of several de-
nominations shown in
the cells

Old Ben Coal at Steeleville:
the seams opened and ground
pulled back into spoil heaps—
TRESPASSERS WILL BE
PROSECUTED

                        south,
sniffers and choked buzzbox
in the mines; the measure of coal
dust—"I am a Christian man.
I have nothing to hide."

5   Q. Have you heard of inmates able to break cuffs open with

6   their own hands, by the force of their hands?

7   A. No, sir. I have heard of inmates who could slip the

8   handcuffs by kind of compressing or dislocating their bones,

9   their fingers. I don't recall reading of an inmate who by

10   just super-strength broke the wrist connection.*

---

* The United States of America v. Usama bin Laden et al (defendants including Khalfan Khamis Mohamed). Defense attorney David Ruhnke deposing Dr. Mark Cunningham, a clinical and forensic psychologist in private practice. June 26, 2001.

Song of Three Jonesboro Girls in a Field

"How we learned to dance the reel. The
lines formed in that Bone Gap gymnasium.
Us, skinny virgins on this side. Taller ones in
the fold-out bleachers. A man said, 'Dance!'"

"And I said, 'Do you know who you're
talking to, old man? My mother made love
to that black cloud, Zeus.' He said, 'I don't
mean nothin' by it. I just play the field.'"

"What were we to say to that? Pick your
own plot, old man? Gather your own stones?
Pay the fiddler, then head out back. Boys
there, drinking uncut booze from paper cups."

(PREACHER:

tragedy
has again
stalked across
our smiling
fields and green
country
   lanes   once
more fear casts
her pall and grips
the hearts of our
citizens *

---

* The Rev. Kent Dale (First Christian Church; Fairfield, Illinois) at the funeral of Roy Shelton, shot off his tractor on June 7, 1950.

Sites are specific, all right, we
inhabit them and go on—

the "B" Deck   Panther
Creek mine #2   somewhere
in the air over gunfire
along the Illinois Central
tracks   waiting
                              you, Karl

like some "Black Charlie" Harris
in a car full of men you carved
the place out of yourself intricate
city in your tunings in the German
words themselves

                              Was it the land?
The men around you? The violences
passing through your arms and back?
Despite Augusta's claims, there are no
palpable Cossacks on Indiana Avenue.

the people are moving   West
Frankfort just a crossroads then
the Ukrainian, Hungarian, and
Italian miners up from the 'bama
hill country   41,000 by 1929
strikes in '29 and '32 and smoke-
less rock struck in West Virginia
men out of work 2-6 yrs rumors
of Communists and strikebreakers

.

Where then, Karl?

the Iron Cross for bravery
in combat (no one else would
go up, artillery-spotting in a balloon,
you said) some union business   you,
the radio, and Augusta, eating cherries
from a green plastic bowl something
about a lawyer

               I'm tryin' to establish
a pattern of behavior here!

                        The lawyer's
words or yours? Where, in or out of place?
the long kitchen reeking of half-cooked
onion and burned potatoes left by the men
last night   Chrysler Imperial backseat—
children asking, "What did you do in the
jazz age, Grandpa?"

                    place is nothing

the banks in Herrin and Johnston
City undergoing "examination and
readjustment" thousands of farms
returned to scrub oak *he salvaged*
tipple and a gasoline engine and
went into a gopher hole those en-
trenched or stranded in Eldorado
living on "doubling up" or Red
Cross flour   *not even the TVA*

but another version of the question, there's
no answer

        But then which were you?
The soldier in the photograph? The Kaiser's
gray muscle? Old man feeding watermelon to
his granddaughter? *melting, pink chunks,*
child's lip giving way Augusta tending garden,
her tomatoes and golden lady slippers. Where
was the shotgun?

        Milk bottles are ex-
ploding across the Midwest and I'm helpless
to stop them. Root cellars collapsing under
weight of so many preserves. Renegade
speeding away in his old Imperial.

        (by reputation:
                I know him. He'll do.

or imagining a Fourth of
July parade at Carrier Mills
or Ziegler not cars leaving
Oklahoma but ex-miners on
benches or marching with
flags *just the WPA going on
now* not even the promise
of that growing national
defense initiative

                    (why did they stay?

the utter chaos of the
scene Paradise and String-
town   chip seal sown
sun on an Impala's
hood four miles from
here *the passionate being*
prepares his explosions and
exploits in this solitude

bridge too low to dive
from rust and silt pressed into
concrete "a grit of occasion"
car radio sings *she'd drag me*

through the streets of Balti-
more   this span of no use
river summers in its right-
hand channel   wheel slips
against mud   *I got some money*

'cause I just got paid   you grin,
Karl royal flycatcher hogleg
in your back pocket   boxhead
rises in the mud   your voice
eddies   prairie dock and purple
cone flowers along the tracks

We could resort to *homeplace* and
birth, talk about being *strangers*
and *pilgrims*, but the poem won't do
voices. The story is stranded upriver.
Not some land that I lost, but lost *you*
there, Karl. You slipped through the
history, unrecognized and unfollowed.
Without notes or headlines. Only
rumors of an explosion. Said "Karl":
I've never been down there.

But what if it was the wrong train, Karl?
The wrong woman?

                              And throwing
your voice, juggling dynamite at the
church picnic—who would miss a stick
or two? And true, that preacher from
St. John's probably needed a punch in
the nose. But your sons, dancing with
those girls from the Levee? Then cruising
out past the power plant at the lake. You
not even noting the lace or weeds in road-
side ditches. Junk collected by the eye while
driving. Stan Mikita passing to Pit Martin.
Goldslip of candy wrapper. *Onslaught of*
commonplace.

the sheep on the wall
the woman in the front seat
the cop on the ground
he careth for you

Displacements occur? Enact? Introduced
to his executioner, Charlie Birger said,
"It *is* a beautiful world." Certain names,
waters charted or mapped. The derailed coal
train. *The utter chaos of the scene.* Weeds
against sky. Earl Shelton dead in his sleep.
Something about a lawyer. *Some other spring.*
Or questions. These grasses are moving. Who
started these rumors of history? Do you find
the violences redemptive? Is a single channel
evident? *Then propositions.* If a man has
property, he must be sane. Sassafras roots
will not hold the subsoil. A road south.
Destination's important to me. But place?
The world begins in a ditch.

NOTES ON THE FOUND TEXTS OF "BLUE MOUND TO 161"

Accounts of the murder of strikebreakers and company guards of the Southern Illinois Coal Company near Herrin are drawn from Paul Angle's *Bloody Williamson* (Urbana: University of Illinois Press, 1952). Angle's accounts also describe the efforts of S. Glenn Young and the Klan to eliminate bootleggers and gamblers from the area in the 1920's. Malcolm Brown and John Webb tell the story of the region's economic and social disintegration in the first part of the century in *Seven Stranded Coal Towns* (Washington: WPA Monograph Series, 1941). On the Shelton gang, Taylor Pensoneau's *Brothers Notorious* (New Berlin: Downstate Publications, 2002) was also very helpful.

Identifications and descriptions of weeds, grasses, and wildflowers are made with the help of *A Flora of Southern Illinois* by R.H. Mohlenbrock and J.W. Voigt (Carbondale: Southern Illinois University Press, 1959). Information on soils and populations from the Illinois Department of Natural Resources was also extremely helpful. The account of the botanists' field trip is taken from Edgar Anderson's *Plants, Man, and Life* (Boston: Little, Brown and Company, 1952).

Private Kern's diary of the journey to kidnap Vice President Andrew Johnson is anthologized within *Guerillas on the Mississippi* by L.E.A. Graham and John Q. Breedlove (Charleston: Bromios Press, 1974).

For riffs on the relationship of place and geography, I am indebted to Michael Anania's *In Natural Light* (Wakefield, R.I.: Asphodel Press, 1999), C.S. Giscombe's *Into and Out of Dislocation* (New York: North Point Press, 2000) and *Here* (Normal: Dalkey Archive Press, 1994), Philip Jenks' *On the Cave You Live In* (Chicago: Flood Editions, 2002), Lisa Robertson's "How Pastoral: A Manifesto" from *Telling It Slant* (eds. Mark Wallace and Steven Marks; Tuscaloosa: University of Alabama Press, 2002), translations from *The Homeric Hymns* done by Charles Boer (Chicago: Swallow Press, 1970), and *Exploring the Land and Rocks of Southern Illinois* by Stanley Harris, C. William Horrell, and Daniel Irwin (Carbondale: Southern Illinois University Press, 1977).